This book is dedicated to all of the dedicated teachers around the world.

The noblest profession on the planet is that of a teacher.
This profession provides unparalleled prestige.
Although we do not receive the recognition, pay, or admiration we deserve, our efforts are reflected in the success of our students.
This book is for you if you take pride in your profession.
If you're feeling down, this book is for you.
This book is for you if you are conflicted, and it is also for you if you are ready to take on the great challenge of navigating a classroom.

Contents

Here's a poem to get you started: v
What kind of educator do you consider yourself to be? 1
Teaching the holistic child (DEI framework) 7
Parental Involvement 15
Indispensable classroom experiences: How to leverage technology. 23
Data-driven instruction 27
Leveraging veteran pedagogues 31
Classroom Management 35
How to avoid burnout 39
There is gratification in this profession 43
Teaching is a calling, NOT a job 45
Works Cited 47

Here's a poem to get you started:

"Those Who Created Themselves"

The coats of power are worn on the backs of
those who have received knowledge.
They are the earth's movers and shakers.
They have the ability to captivate a generation in ways
that previous generations could not have imagined.
Every day, they bless people by granting
them access to holiness.
The pursuit of self-discovery leads to holiness.
Their greatness is truly realized when the
formatted ideas of their students are illuminated
on scales that outweigh their teachings.
Keep that in mind!
That priceless gem!
Activate your calling!
Your body is limited in comparison to your calling,
which is greatness, just as greatness is to your existence.
The similarities between the present and the future are
indistinguishable; they must first meet on the journey's boat.
Don't worry; Life is the captain, and
he will get you there safely.
Location is evocation.
Time and prime aren't always compatible,
but when are, the result is savory.

What kind of educator do you consider yourself to be?

ALTHOUGH THE LANDSCAPE of teaching and learning has changed dramatically (in both good and bad ways) as educators, we must adapt and keep effective learning and teaching at the forefront of our efforts.

Consider a classroom to be a safe haven. Healing, reflection, acceptance, and solidarity should be all present in this space.

A classroom is a revelation hub with the same virtues and mysticism as a temple, and it, too, is a sacred space for learning and teaching.

A teacher's vision is equal to the greatness of his or her students.

Students' importance is a direct result of their teachers 'modulating and healing abilities in bringing them back to "self." Bringing a student to "self" is a one-of-a-kind, doable, and sacred process that necessitates vision, patience, deliberateness, and craft mastery. Bringing a person to "self" is the ability to walk them through the process of discovering their true selves. I recall having teachers who challenged my assumptions about the world or about things I believed to be true solely because my culture or family taught me so. When a student is able to interrogate their own thinking in response to your instruction and possibly perform and render a different analysis than their previous one, this brings a student to "self." This is not simple, but it is possible. Like doves, young people already have wings—wings of ability, intelligence, and willingness—but how a teacher uses those wings makes all the difference.

Children are complete humans with abilities that have not yet been fine-tuned, excavated, or realized. The truth is that being a teacher isn't so much about what you know as what you don't know about yourself and others, and how the learning environment can help reveal what you need to know about yourself and others (students). This is why this line of work must be treated with reverence.

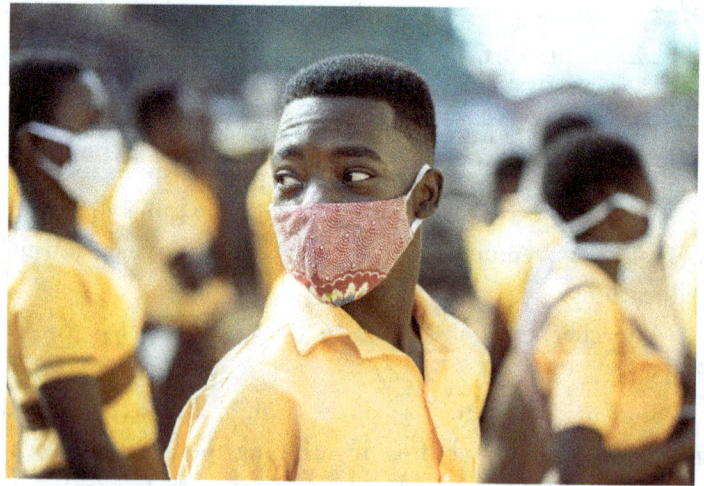

There's something majestic about an enlightened mind, but the process and the healer (teacher) who facilitates that enlightenment are even more profound.

The first time I walked into a classroom, I was nervous, excited, naive, and full of zeal. See, the old adage is true: teaching is an art, not a science. Because young minds are both vulnerable and valuable assets in society, how they are educated in schools is critical. Teaching gives you a sense of power and accomplishment.

As a teacher, I have the ability to change people's minds, hearts, and focus, but most importantly, I have the ability to set a generation on the path to success. My desire to become an English teacher stemmed from my love of reading. I reasoned that because I enjoy reading, I could teach English. I was mistaken. Teaching entails much more than simply imparting content knowledge. Teaching is about having a heart, having a purpose, being flexible, being tolerant, and searching your soul.

Being pliable, accessible, compassionate, and a healer are all important qualities in this profession. When students enter the classroom, they do so with the intention of experiencing and exploring life's possibilities.

> ## *Here's the Nugget*
>
> Teachers and students must collaborate to create a sense of community in the learning environment. The teacher is the leader, while the students are future leaders. Because the leader is the body's head and if the head moves, the body moves, the leader must be intentional or else the entire body will move unintentionally, which can have negative consequences.

To consider how and why we teach is crucial.

One of the most violent aspects of today's education is deficit teaching. Deficit teaching occurs when educators state that students are unable or unwilling to do something without acknowledging students' talents and skills that can be used in the learning space to enhance established skills while learning new ones. Essentially, deficit teaching focuses on problems rather than potential.

Throughout my years of teaching, I've heard both experienced and inexperienced teachers say the same thing: "They can't read." "They don't read at grade level." My heart sinks as a parent and a teacher when I hear this.

Look, I'm sure I've said something similar in the past but here's why these statements are so threatening: Teaching and learning are shaped by social and cultural factors.

Students who struggle to read a sentence aren't necessarily dunces; what if we consider that they haven't yet uncovered that ability? Our entire teaching approach will change from negative to positive.

I taught a journalism class to a group of 8th graders at a charter school in Brooklyn. I thought it would be fascinating for them to observe young people's struggles all over the world, so I showed them a video of young children harvesting cocoa beans in Brazil and Western Africa for large chocolate companies in Belgium. How many of you enjoy chocolate? That was my hook for the lesson. Are you aware of the origins of your chocolate?

I recall students asking, "Why, Miss?" before we started watching the video.

I went on to say, "How would you feel if you knew that young people your age and younger were forced into child labor to harvest the beans that produced the lovely chocolate bars you adore?"

They responded:

> "What?"
> "No, Miss! You're joking, right?"
> "Is this something that happens?"
> "Are you attempting to deceive us?"
> "But, oh well!"
> "They don't pay them, Miss?"
> "What exactly does this have to do with us, Miss?"

Because of my student's emotional intelligence and/or awareness, the responses varied. Investigating this heinous reality can serve as a teaching opportunity. As teachers, especially literacy teachers, we must recognize that teaching and learning can serve as a portal for social and political engagement and change.

"Education is a formidable force," Mandela said. A force can be used for both good and bad. Young minds have limitless potential, but it takes a skilled classroom instructor to bring out their full potential.

After I showed them the video, we had a Socratic seminar to discuss what we saw and how we felt about it. The casual responses ranged from *what's the big deal!* and *I don't give a damn!* to *wow, Ms. Anderson, that's awful! You're the only one of our teachers who teaches us things like this!*

I specified these responses for a reason. This example isn't just about my joy; it's also about the changes that young minds undergo when the classroom serves and informs them.

In the video, a boy lived with his grandmother after both of his parents died of HIV.

He was between the ages of ten and twelve. Despite that he didn't go to school, his intelligence was evident throughout the film. For example, when it was time for dinner, he would go bird hunting. First, he would boil wild cherries until they turn into a paste. Then he would spread the paste along riverbanks where birds came to drink.

The birds would become stuck in the glue, and he would roast them for himself and his grandmother. My students deduced that, while this young man didn't know how to write a paragraph, his intelligence was obvious, and one could argue that he may outperform many first-world students.

Learning and teaching are two sides of the same coin. Teachers who enter classrooms with the illusion of omnipotence are not only violent in practice but unprepared to teach.

Every day, I learn something new from my students. I pick up new words and ways of thinking about things. Seeing the world through the eyes of children and teenagers enlightens me in ways that my adulthood cannot. My students' technological ability and savviness are out of this world. In my classrooms, I've seen graphic designers, computer engineers, and data strategists eager to be discovered.

> ### Here's the nugget
>
> Facilitate a classroom that is student-centered, joyous, informative, and celebratory; a space where mistakes and growth happen.

Teaching the holistic child (DEI framework)

YOUNG PEOPLE CRAVE structure, consistency, and discipline.

Most teachers believe that their content knowledge distinguishes them as excellent educators. This is incorrect. Among the characteristics of a great teacher are the ability to bring a child to the brink of self-actualization, purpose, and self-awareness. A student can learn content from anyone and anywhere (Internet, friend, family, etc.). Delivery and facilitation skills set great pedagogues apart from the rest.

I've learned that if children aren't emotionally ready, they won't be ready academically. Academic unavailability is frequently misinterpreted as unruly and difficult.

Why do some students give some teachers a hard time?

Your students don't dislike *you;* they are testing the teacher's approach, which causes the teacher to recalibrate in order to better serve the students or restore their expectations.

I most enjoy working with those students who are stubborn or resistant. As a teacher, my job is to groom and develop students. Education, like teaching and learning, is a process.

Teachers must become acquainted with their students. I recommend conducting a quarterly personality assessment of students. Make room for social connections and commonalities. When teachers connect with their students, the learning environment becomes more enjoyable and effective. It's important to get to know the people you're teaching. In reality, as educators, we wield more power than their parents. We can frequently introduce them to concepts beyond their awareness through content, so knowing them and establishing a relationship with them is a no-brainer for the learning experience.

For example, I tell students about my academic experience, my family, my life, and my objectives—within the scope of what is appropriate and efficacious, of course. While maintaining boundaries and discipline, I humanize myself. Humanizing myself is important because it allows my students to feel comfortable making mistakes while also showing them that, in many cases, I am just like them. I make errors. I can reflect on and learn from my past experiences, for example.

Some teachers don't connect with students outside of the classroom. I share my lunch with students and tell them family jokes so they can see how similar we are. One of my favorite conversations with students is talking about how parents don't understand. I tell them I was a rambunctious adolescent, that as a kid I thought I knew everything, but life had other ideas.

I recall instructing a historical fiction class. The Civil Rights Movement was the focus of the original curriculum. I persuaded my supervisor that I needed to do something different.

Prior to writing their stories, I decided to have my students research the Haitian Revolution, the Cuban Revolution, the Morant Bay Rebellion, and the Grenadian Revolution. We spent a week researching these places, watching videos, going on gallery walks, etc. Students who barely paid attention in other classes became enthralled:

> "Miss, my family is from there!"
> "Miss, that's something my mother told me in Haiti!"
> "Miss, my family is from Jamaica, so I'm very interested in learning about this!"

To educate students, we must seek ways to connect with them.

"Black children who are bored and unengaged may behave in ways that are disruptive or may simply stop participating," writes Debra Ren-Etta Sullivan in *Cultivating* the *Genius* of *Black Children*. Most children, Sullivan continues, will engage in a learning environment if learning is presented in ways that:

> make sense to them;
> make learning natural and enjoyable; and
> make learning relevant.

The intriguing aspect of Sullivan's claim is that it applies to all students. I would be remiss, however, if I grouped all students and ignored the distinct plight of black and brown students in terms of disengagement and teachers' inadequate responses to these students.

As a learner, if I don't find meaning in a learning environment, my interest will natural fade. Young people are subject to the same concept. It is the teacher's responsibility to pique and maintain a student's interest. Yes, some topics are more fascinating than others, but it's important to remember that hooking students entails more than simply exposing them to interesting topics. To keep students engaged, the classroom should include a variety of activities.

Let's face it, whether in college or high school, we've all had those moments when we couldn't wait for class to end because the environment didn't provide us with the "Oomph" we were looking for—whatever that was. That it factor that we were missing as students is what we need to provide in our classrooms. To leverage a cavernous element of joy in the learning space, we must be spontaneous, creative, and consistent. If we don't do these things, we'll undoubtedly have problems in class.

Dr. Gholdy Muhammad outlined four frameworks for cultivating brilliant minds in her book *Cultivating Genius*: identity, skills, intellectualism, and criticality. I'm going to use these frameworks to help students create inspiring classrooms.

To begin, we need to recognize that we must teach young people to know who they are if they are to make sense of life on a larger scale as well as navigate the various systems in which they live and operate. One of the mistakes schools make, particularly in history classes, is to teach students about different types of systems and governments without also teaching them how to dismantle and reimagine ineffective systems. For example, when I taught a high school government course a few years ago, my objective was to cover what was in the scope and sequence. I regurgitated how systems work or worked, and I tested students' understanding. In retrospect, I should have spent more time teaching them how to reshape and dismantle anything they found unfair or outdated.

One of the goals of education is to allow young minds to stretch beyond what is considered normal. Are we going to teach students to conform to societal norms or to defy the canons of the educational status quo? This is the conundrum we face as educators. These are issues that we must all address.

For me, the answer is straightforward. We need to create spaces that allow young minds to think beyond the social and educational framework of simply knowing things but also doing something with that knowledge. Empowerment does not come from mere knowledge. The goal is to combine knowledge with action.

To me, "empowerment education" entails providing students with information that allows them to take action and reflect on what it means to be a global citizen—which is exactly what Dr. Gholdy Muhammad explains in her book. Young people require mastery of content-area and grade-level skills, as well as the space and opportunity to critically examine their own learning. For example: What did I learn in Ms. Anderson's class, and, most importantly, how can I apply what I learned in science, math, and social studies? This approach is referred to as interdisciplinary education.

"Democracy functions most effectively when people from different backgrounds interact, communicate their interests, and participate in shaping the purposes by which they live," says Diane Ravitch.

Many of us work alone as teachers. Our content, like our approach, is isolated; when teachers work alone, they are not serving their students' best interests. In fact, how students interpret and navigate the learning environment is influenced by this solitary approach. Teaching in a vacuum, in my opinion, is pedagogical malpractice.

"Each one teach one"[1]* is a method that every educator should and must follow in order to master this art.

---

1   *"Each one teach one," a phrase from slavery times when slaves were not allowed to learn to read, urged each person who learned to read to teach another.

Many of our students are able to express their social dissatisfactions, particularly in light of the recent increase in police violence against black people. They do not, however, have any concrete plans to address these issues. Dr. Muhammad discusses the importance of verbal and written expression around these issues, as well as how important it is for young people to be able to empower themselves in such a way that they not only understand the dynamics of power and oppression, but also position themselves to improve anti-oppression sentiments among themselves in order to change society's landscape. This necessitates action. It depends on what that looks like. For instance, if you despise sentencing guidelines, you could work as a prosecutor, judge, or district attorney. Participate in educational policy so that the educational system can be changed.

Student engagement is unavoidable when content is meaningful and relevant.

Teachers who fail to update outdated curriculums in order to facilitate and teach holistically are failing their students. Educational environments should be relevant, rigorous, and memorable. Education should broaden the scope and potential of a person's life.

> **HERE'S THE NUGGET**
>
> Every child in the classroom deserves to be affirmed. Classrooms should be safe havens. Students must feel connected to the content. The nuggets have more power as individual Statement.

Parental Involvement

MOST PARENTS WANT a positive relationship with their children's teachers. Some parents are educators in their own right.

All parents want the same traits in their children's teachers:

- an effective teacher;
- a compassionate teacher;
- an accessible teacher;
- a candid teacher.

Every teacher desires the same traits in their students' parent(s):

- an engaged parent(s);
- a collaborative parent(s);
- a reachable parent(s);
- a responsive parent(s).

As teachers, we must recognize that parents are the best experts in regard to their children, so using parental knowledge is critical in us teaching them. I believe a parent/teacher class should be required in all schools. In this class, parents would come to understand the school's True North—our beliefs, values, and principles—which is important because parents are often cut off from the school community when it comes to what their children are learning in the classroom. Aside from parent-teacher conferences and bad phone calls home, most parents are unaware of what is going on in the classroom. This lack of involvement must be changed. Parents should be expected to participate in their child's learning.

Numerous parents who have made an effort to participate have said to me: Ms. Anderson, "I'm not sure what to expect."

This participation requirement is mainly to ensure that parents understand the school's curriculum.

The goal of a parent/teacher class is to strengthen the teacher-parent relationship while advancing the school's mission.

Schools should maintain a consistent outreach program. Before a student matriculates in the school, the dangers of absenteeism and non-contactable students should be discussed. Parents must understand that if their child does not follow the school's attendance rules and policy, the school community will not be able to help their child reach his or her full potential, which is one of our ultimate goals. I believe that fostering this type of relationship between schools and homes holds all parties accountable for the child/ren's success or lack thereof. The future of a student is a collaborative effort between home and school.

How to handle difficult parents

Consider what constitutes a difficult parent or parents:

- parents who appear disinterested in their children's education;
- parents who are unable to communicate effectively;
- parents who take their child's words at face value;
- non-responsive parents.

Parents, like teachers, are human beings. They deal with life's issues, so a teacher/parent relationship is often a parent's last priority. Other parents, however, can be difficult.

"If I am the child's parent, it is my obligation and my high duty to civilize the child," writes James Baldwin in "A Talk to Teachers."[2] That children begin learning at home about socialization and how to present themselves is important. Self-respect, respect for others, attention to detail, how to navigate the dynamics of authority, and how to follow rules are a few of the basic principles that we should all learn from our parents/homes. Yet many of our students have not had the opportunity or the financial means to experience these rites of passage, so the classroom is an excellent place to cultivate these skills. For this reason, in my opinion, a teacher is a second parent.

Parents, like students, must feel a bond with their children's teachers. Always address a parent with the phrase or in the spirit of *I am your child's second parent.* I teach and interact with this mindset. Most parents appreciate this approach. To love young people is

---

2   Baldwin, J. (2008). A talk to teachers. *Yearbook of the National Society for the Study of Education, 107*(2), 15-20. Doi: 10.1111/j.1744-7984.2008.00154.x

easy because, since the future belongs to them, the responsibility for shaping their minds is a sacred opportunity. Call to update parents on their child's day; tell them that their child worked hard on a test and you've noticed significant improvements, etc.. Don't contact parents solely to complain. Complaining is a turnoff that fosters resentment and interferes with the parent-teacher relationship.

Parents don't know what they don't know—that is, parents must be informed that you are their child's advocate. *You* have a stake in their success, and *you* want to see their children reach their full potential both inside and outside the classroom.

> ### Here's the nugget
>
> Parents are an important part of the stakeholder pie; they want to be involved, they need support, and some parents need to shift their focus they require assistance, which the school community must always be willing to provide.

How to handle administrative challenges

Most administrators once worked as classroom teachers, so most administrators fight for their teachers. Others are far removed from that experience and act accordingly.

I've never managed a school, but I imagine it's difficult to delegate and accommodate different personalities and expectations. As a result, administrators and teachers must extend grace toward one another.

Why do some administrators and teachers fall out?

Among the numerous reasons for this type of tension, ego and miscommunication are the most common.

Regardless of position, everyone has the same goal in mind: student success. When each side's vision is realized differently, tension arises.

Some teachers argue that their ideas aren't taken seriously.

Some administrators believe that some teachers are incapable of being coached.

Everyone, regardless of position, can be coached.

Nowadays, teaching consists primarily of performative activities[3] and paperwork. However, teachers spend more time preparing and filling out Google docs and spreadsheets than they do teaching.

Among the complaints about administration I've heard teachers voice over the years are:

- Administrators don't value my contribution to the team;
- A lack of transparency exists regarding promotions and bonuses;
- Feedback is inadequate;
- Administrators fail to provide adequate pedagogical support.

Among the complaints I've heard in leadership meetings are:

- Some of these teachers just want to complain;

---

3 As a performative act, a teacher's words and actions aim to effect cognitive, affective, and behavioral changes in learners. (W. Mark Liew, 2013).

- Teachers don't know how to adapt;
- Teachers want to run the school.

All of the above are partially true, but methodology is the problem.

Inexperienced and unfit leadership are in teachers is among the most concerning issues plaguing today's schools, particularly those in urban areas. Many schools are operated by leaders with less than five years of classroom experience. If you haven't mastered the ins and outs of educational quarters, how can you expect others to?

In addition, nepotism is a serious problem in schools. Most schools have cliques of teachers and leaders who look out for one another.

Administrators must avoid favoritism among teachers. I've been in meetings where teachers have complained that they haven't received any feedback on their lessons or been observed teaching in weeks, despite their prior observation reports being inadequate. Others brag about always receiving useful feedback. This state of affairs should not be the case.

Open communication between teachers and administrators is one way to circumvent the gap. Teachers and administrative professionals must understand that the ultimate goal is to improve the lives of the students they serve. Both parties must be aware of the difficulties that come with the job.

The school will fail if there are no teachers, especially good teachers.

The school will fail if it does not have an effective and strong leadership team.

Teachers and administrators are similar to columns in a building; if one of the columns fails, the entire structure is in serious danger of collapsing.

Teachers and administrators can't serve without each other.

Danger ensues when administrators don't know the curriculum or their students.

I've worked in schools where the principals were either too far away from the classroom to model what they were asking of me as a teacher, or they couldn't model it themselves.

Some principals are unaware of a content area's scope and sequence. Why? Curricula knowledge should be a stipulation. When you don't know or understand what I'm teaching, how can you give me effective feedback or a quality review?

How can you give teachers a thorough evaluation when you spend less than twenty minutes observing in their classroom twice a year?

The phrase "This is my school" is among the worst a principal can say.

No, it is not *your* school; it is *our* school—and there is no school without teachers.

"It's my classroom and my rules" is among the worst phrases a teacher can say.

Yes, you should have the freedom to make your own rules, but, in any school, uniformity is essential. To effectively serve young people, both leadership and teachers must unite in their approach.

A leadership position should not impair your moral judgment, and teaching should not diminish your respectability.

Danger ensues when teachers are unequipped and lack intellectual preparation.

I've worked with unfit colleagues who had no idea what they were doing in the classroom. Students came into my English classroom and asked me about algebra, a subject I don't teach and with which I am unfamiliar with the scope and sequence of the curriculum. Students told me that the teacher was unfamiliar with the work they were assigning. Why? A teacher's lack of subject understanding is unacceptable.

As educators, we must prepare our lessons, go over our teaching points, and, if necessary, practice our presentations as educators.

> How can we teach if we don't know what we're talking about?
>
> How can we teach if we don't have a plan for answering questions and navigating the lesson?
>
> How can we teach if we don't have a model with which to compare student work?

As teachers, we must know what we're looking for if we are to provide quality feedback.

We must have criteria for determining if the lesson was successful with a clear beginning, middle, and end. Collected data determines whether we need to reteach, etc.

> ### Here's the Nugget
>
> There's only one goal but many paths to reach that goal; each side must be willing to see the other's point of view.

Indispensable classroom experiences: How to leverage technology

MANY OF US were caught off guard when Covid struck. Although we were aware of Google Classroom, we had never used it.

Many of us were apprehensive. We posed questions like:

How will I keep students engaged online?
What's the best way for me to share my screen?
What's the best way to make breakout rooms?
How do I maintain a sense of joy?

To help us engage our students, we used Zoom, Loom, Google Classroom, Kahoot!, Google Meet, Pear Deck, and a variety of other tools.

At first, many of us found it difficult to navigate technology. However, Covid taught us the value of technology and the critical role it plays in our students' education. For teachers to claim that they are unfamiliar with a platform is no longer acceptable. To engage our students. it is our responsibility to attend professional developments on a given platform. Because the majority of students are technologically savvy, we must meet them through technology. Age and inexperience are no longer acceptable excuses for teachers to avoid technology.

During the pandemic, I learned how to record lessons with Loom and upload them to Google Classroom so that students could still access teacher instructions. I enjoyed the experience, as should we all, because it adds an additional layer of accessibility and support to pandemic teaching. In fact, I believe that in the coming decade, technology will be at the center of large-scale learning and teaching. Now that our lives are returning to normal with in-person learning, again the norm, it is up to us teachers to take everything we've learned about online learning and apply it to physical classrooms.

First and foremost, each classroom should be a welcoming, joyful, and a safe, stable, supportive, and vibrant Zen-like environment.

In a learning environment, students and teachers should form an unbreakable bond. There should be a sense of urgency, agency, and joy when students walk into a classroom. A child cannot learn if the teacher is constantly irritated, if peers fight, and if the classroom has no walls, to name a few examples. Furthermore, a child cannot and should not be expected to learn solely from a computer. Learning should be a mix of the two, e.g., we can complete our "Do Now" on a Google form, and the teacher can display the results on the smartboard eliciting debates and discussions, especially if the lesson requires it.

Over the years, I've had students who initially disliked me, but by the end of the first week, I'd become their favorite teacher. This happened because they felt connected to me, understood me, and I gave them agency by listening to them, respecting them, and believing in them.

I recall a student who had a reputation for being troubled. When she arrived in my class. I inquired as to her favorite color. That threw her off guard:

"Why do you ask, Miss? No one has ever asked about that!"

"I'm just curious."
"Pink," she said.
"I despise the color pink."
"Why? You can combine pink with other colors, you know…"

I connected with her right away because I tapped into her emotions. We began taking pictures, and she asked where I grew up, which I told her. During our conversation, we discovered that we shared the same culture (Jamaican). She was overjoyed. She regularly caused me problems, but she never crossed the line into disrespecting me. Even when she didn't show my coworkers courtesy, she always reserved that ounce of respect for me. I encouraged her and held her accountable for repeatedly disrespecting my peers. My point with this example, which is one of my many, is that in teaching young people, relationship building and connectivity are critical.

> ### HERE'S THE NUGGET
>
> Allow your students to put their faith in you. Teaching topics to students has to have a reason. Students will become disengaged if the topic is not intriguing.

Data-driven instruction

- How do you keep track of student progress?
- What effect does teaching style have on student achievement?

TEACHERS ARE FREQUENTLY bound by a pacing calendar that limits their ability to stretch or extend some teaching points. Every lesson must have order and expectations, but it is counterproductive if teachers rush through lessons to stick to the pacing calendar rather than ensure that students are learning the skills and competencies they require. When this happens, our schools become a jumble of superficial ideas.

Teachers must keep track of what their students are learning as well as any gaps in their knowledge and the steps taken to close them.

It is critical to conduct assessments (formative, summative, etc.) If data isn't used to inform instruction, the teacher will be teaching blindly. Teaching blindness is risky because it causes regression in those who need to learn new skills and difficulties for those who require remedial assistance.

I propose that teachers create skill and participation trackers to keep track of their students' progress. This is critical because it not only assists the teacher in guiding his or her instructions, but also enables students to determine their exact location within the content area. The majority of students want to know where they are in their learning, and when a teacher is able to provide them with a thorough and tangible analysis of where they are, but most importantly, show them where they need to be and how to get there, it empowers them on numerous levels. Indeed, this level of transparency can catapult the student to greatness.

Many students are able to articulate their thoughts verbally but struggle to write them. We must explicitly teach the abilities required for genius to shine in both written and verbal communication. As a secondary teacher, I am not afraid to revisit fundamental skills. I teach and review sentence structures, homophones, fragments, and subject verb agreement in my AP courses. While I may be perceived as the teacher who crosses all the T's and dots all the I's, I recognize the importance of a holistic approach and thus do what is necessary rather than complain about gaps and inabilities.

Additionally, teachers can collaborate across disciplines and analyze this data. Every subject area requires some level of written proficiency. For instance, in mathematics, providing a numerical breakdown is insufficient; students are required to justify their answers. Students are required to provide rationales for their responses. The point? All teachers must use data to teach students and assess their work.

In contrast, some schools have adopted a pernicious practice that sets a large number of students up for failure: these schools rely heavily on standardized and formative assessments as their primary benchmarks. While the educational system accepts that some students will never write an essay on the level of Mark Twain, other ways exist to recognize and celebrate these students' academic intelligence to meet the benchmark. Many schools now assess students through performance tasks. This alternate method is wonderful because it enables students to create items that center on their passions and demonstrate their aptitude. If a student is able to recreate an actual play after reading it, rather than writing an elaborate essay about it, I believe it is better for them to recreate rather than struggle with something formal like an essay. Indeed, recreation necessitates higher level thought and application, which are necessary life skills. This is what I mean when I refer to empowerment learning. Students crave interactions, and interactions breed pride, and when a student can demonstrate their pride in developing something, their self-esteem soars to new heights. Again, this is what it means to reconnect a student with his or her "self."

> ### *Here's the nugget*
>
> While data is critical, one size does not fit all; we must adjust, adapt, and recalibrate to capture all of the talents present in a learning environment.

Leveraging veteran pedagogues

"AN OLD BROOM knows every nook and cranny."
Unknown

This quotation is ideal for illustrating why it makes sense for new pedagogues to team up with veteran teachers who have a lot of nuggets. Many schools, in my experience, have mentorship or fellowship programs that allow a new teacher to work with a veteran teacher for a year.

A veteran teacher can provide a new teacher with insight into the school's culture, students, and colleagues. Veteran teachers can assist new teachers in avoiding common pitfalls. Teachers who have taught for a long time are aware of which strategies work and which do not—especially in their schools.

As a teacher, having a collaborative spirit is essential because you will feel like a fish out of water if you don't. Teachers collaborate to share resources. One of the most important things a new teacher needs is access to resources.

For a new teacher to get a sense of the environment is crucial. Don't jump in with both feet. To establish professional trust is also crucial. I advise new teachers to develop professional relationships with their colleagues so that they will know who to contact if they are in need of assistance. Avoid being a lone wolf, as this will not serve you; also, avoid becoming too involved until you have identified your niche and a firm grasp on the school's dynamics. Protect your professional reputation and look for growth opportunities without ruffling anyone's feathers. In your interactions with colleagues and students, use both emotional and logical judgments. Concentrate on our primary objective, which is to educate and elevate young people.

Joining the teachers' disgruntled gossip club is professional suicide and one of the deadliest mistakes I've seen new teachers make. Seniority is crucial because a behavior in a teacher who has worked at a school for ten to fifteen years may be tolerated, whereas that same behavior in a new teacher may result in that teacher's being disciplined or fired. Furthermore, gossiping is detrimental to one's career. Focus your ideas and use your skillsets to improve what needs to be improved. The sad reality of today's schools is that everyone is disposable. You can't rely on your talent alone to keep you safe. In my opinion, flexibility is essential. Make your complaint into a question if you have one. A toxic environment with no real solutions is the last thing administration wants.

Veteran teachers can also learn from new teachers. New teachers bring a sense of spontaneity and passion to the classroom from which veterans can benefit. Also, some new teachers have excellent subject knowledge and, to be honest, in most cases are better trained in social emotional learning.

Allies, collaborators, a strong support system, and flexibility are all essential.

> ### HERE'S THE NUGGET
>
> There is room for both new and veteran teachers, and each group contributes significantly to the education of children. Each group must collaborate to best educate our students.

Classroom Management

I DIDN'T TAKE a single classroom management class in graduate school. Why? Teaching is an art, as I previously stated.
   A new teacher, however, should be trained in some practical and effective strategies. Being a teacher entails being in charge of your classroom. Being an effective manager requires education.

   Prior to acquiring content knowledge, the environment must be conducive to learning. Numerous reports have surfaced since the pandemic of an increase in disruptive behaviors in the classroom. As with adults, young people have been through a great deal as a result of the disruption of learning. Some were unable to access quality instruction online, while others were able to do so. Nonetheless, we must establish systems and procedures that foster respect and accountability. Because no one can learn in a disruptive environment, it is critical to have a defined culture and set of expectations. My belief is that over the last decade, a great deal of emphasis has been placed on SEL (social-emotional learning), which is fantastic, but there has been less emphasis on classroom management. Both of these processes must occur concurrently. We must accommodate young people's emotional states while maintaining rigorous academic and social standards. This is how we truly set them up for success.

There are four different kinds of students:

Pliable

Regardless of content, pliable students respect the learning space. Teachers know that whether or not these students enjoy the subject, they will follow classroom rules and expectations. They may have strict parents/guardians who demand responsibility.

Dos	Don'ts
Provide a consistent compliment, provide incentives, and provide an opportunity for classroom manager roles, etc.	Fail to notice and take for granted

Indecisive

These students tends to follow friends' advice, but they know what's best. They are still figuring out who they are. For them, peer pressure is an issue. They want to be part of the cool crowd, so they cross authority lines, but not too far.

Dos	Don't's
Reiterate expectations from a place of love and care; remind them of their "true" selves and their capabilities.	Punish, compare to others, or threaten parent phone calls.

Resistant

Resistant students intend to cause havoc by any means possible.

Typically from troubled homes, these students have experienced a great deal of trauma. They're looking for a way to connect, but they're using their bad habits to get attention. They yearn for mentors who can relate to them and understand their needs.

Dos	Don't's
Build a relationship with them, hold them accountable, show them love and attention, and look for commonalities.	Use a punitive approach, suspend, ignore, or "adultify."

Strong-headed

Nothing will or can get in the way of these students' concentration.

These students are more likely to come from families who place a high value on education, and their parents are frequently educated as well. These students have long-term goals, such as valedictorian, college, full scholarship, etc.

Dos	Don't's
Offer consistent encouragement, spend time exploring goals, provide resources.	Overlook areas for improvement; praise too often.

All of these students deserve good teachers. But before a teacher can serve his or her students, he or she must first identify them and their personalities. The approach is crucial.

Several years ago, when I was teaching at KIPP in Brooklyn, one of my sixth-graders had an emotional breakdown in the lunchroom. This student was known for his emotional outbursts. I gently pulled the student and held him close as the dean walked over to reprimand him. I hugged the student and told him to relax, that I was there for him. He immediately became less tense, but I could feel his little body trembling with rage as we stood there. My eyes welled up with tears. I sat with him after standing him on his feet. My exact words to him were: "Royal, for me to assist you, you must communicate and refrain from resorting to anger; otherwise, no one will hear you, sweety." He wanted to express his dissatisfaction, so I told him we'd talk about it after lunch.

This is not something I recommend for everyone; do what you believe is best. My point is that sometimes all that is required of a teacher is a "word," reassurance, or a public display of compassion. As educators, it is our responsibility to create an environment conducive to love, compassion, and safety. As a student, I appreciated teachers who made me feel heard, secure, and cared for; I hope to provide similar experiences for my students.

Compassion is essential. We can't serve children as adults or educators if we can't find it in our hearts to see beyond their behavior.

> ### Here's the Nugget
> Knowing who your students are will help you work with them more effectively. To become effective adults, young minds require proper cultivation.

How to avoid burnout

THE RACE ISN'T for the quick, but for those who can finish it. 9:11 Ecclesiastes

Teaching is more than just passion; it's also about purpose. Your passion will change and may fade over time, but your purpose will remain constant. For example, if your needs are no longer met in the classroom, that you will lose interest and enthusiasm is inevitable. What keeps you going as a teacher is the true reason for your job: to assist in the development of tomorrow's leaders. This is where the meaning of life is found.

Working with young people is difficult at times, but it is a necessary profession. Some behaviors are indicative of the fact their brains and socialization skills are still developing. The rule of thumb for educators is to be patient.

Patience is one of the fruits of the teaching spirit. Patience in waiting for students to mature (socially, academically and spiritually). Patience in waiting for them to change. Patience is required to get them through the difficult times.

One of my students, Brandon, had a reputation for being difficult. I had a reputation for being a teacher who taught exciting topics while also being a straight shooter and academically rigorous . Although I taught eighth grade, students in the sixth grade knew my name; my good reputation preceded me. When Brandon walked into my class, I knew I had to strike up a conversation with him right away. He was assigned to me as his mentor as part of a mentorship program. I made it clear that I didn't tolerate drama or disrespect. I described myself as compassionate, communicative, and firm. He gave me a friendly smile and said he had heard about me. Brandon was known for throwing chairs and cursing teachers. He was a hothead with a short fuse. I knew I had to earn his trust and stay by his side even during his meltdowns; however, I always held him accountable.

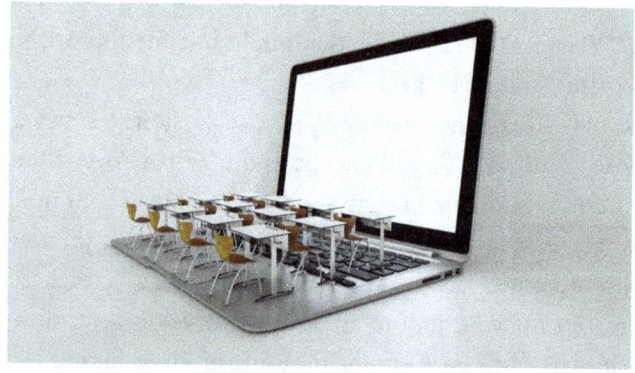

The first time he became upset in my class, I said, "I will not run after you if you leave; also, make sure you finish your work for my class because that is my expectation." He snorted and walked away.

He had my homework and classwork the next day. He'd never done anything like that before. He would occasionally break classroom rules, but not as frequently as he had in seventh grade. Brandon was only with me for a year. If I'd had him longer, I'm sure I could have assisted him in developing new coping mechanisms to deal with his frustrations. I am not bragging about my ability, but rather demonstrating what happens when discipline and compassion are showed. I believe that we all crave discipline, because when structure and discipline are in place, greatness is propelled.

He was on the basketball team and asked if I wanted to come watch him play. I decided to show up unannounced at one of his games. "Wow, Miss Anderson, you really came," he exclaimed when he saw me. I wanted him to know that, despite his behavioral flaws, I still regarded him as a valuable member of my classroom and life. I wanted to maintain a sense of trust and deference. A teacher's purpose is fueled by encounters and examples like these. Nothing is more powerful than a transformed individual. Patience is essential.

Also, this occurred not as a result of me being strict and direct, but because I had already developed a trusting relationship with him outside of academics. He was aware that I cared and that I desired his greatness, but most importantly, he desired greatness for himself. If we were judged in our darkest hours, many of us would not be where we are today. We would exist in a perpetual state of regret. We must extend grace to children and adolescents, and in doing so, we contribute significantly to their development.

> ### *Here's the Nugget*
>
> Teaching necessitates perseverance, steadfastness, and trust, as well as the ability to stay the course in the face of adversity.

There is gratification in this profession

THE TEACHING PROFESSION is the one that creates the others. Teachers have a unique perspective on society and operate differently. I believe that people complain more about our pay and respect than we do, because our work requires both heart and purpose. When we look at children, we see potential for grooming and propelling an individual to greatness. While I'm writing my lesson plans, I'm not thinking about my paycheck; I'm thinking about how my students will interact with the lesson, my stopping points, and assessment, and so on. I'm thinking about my students' futures because that's what I'm most concerned about. The pandemic, in my opinion, elevated the importance of what we do and the fact that what we do should not be taken for granted, but rather exalted and revered.

Teachers, you see, are selfless individuals. We chose this profession because we are passionate about teaching. Grooming the next generation is a noble act.

Although, this profession does not receive the hero worship it deserves in society. It's a prestigious profession. The prestige stems from the high ethical standards that it necessitates.

I encourage my global colleagues to persevere because, while we will continue to seek increased compensation and recognition for our work, the most important factor is the impact we have on young lives, which cannot be quantified.

Teachers are respected members of society.

> ***Here's the nugget***
>
> There is no greater reward than a sparked mind.

Teaching is a calling, NOT a job

A JOB IS a location where you go to trade your labor for money. Teaching is a calling that was placed in your heart long before you realized it.

A teacher exudes a great deal of morality and selflessness that deserves to be recognized and emphasized. Self-discussions are a common part of being a teacher. Great teachers put their hearts and souls into their work; to do so correctly, they must engage in self-reflection and self-evaluation. "Moral decisions are a creative act, connected to a particular state of mind," says Alexander Sidorkin. I agree, but, as an educator, I would go even further and say that my moral functioning is at the heart of what I do. Because my spiritual equilibrium depends on my morality, I must equip myself to act in a righteous manner at all times.

Students rely on their teachers for guidance. A teacher must be available emotionally, academically, and intellectually. If teachers are unable to guide their students in these three areas, the profession's essence is lost. As a result, learning and teaching are impossible. To be clear, when I refer to spirituality, I am not referring to any religion or religious allusion. However, we are spiritual beings operating in a physical world as humans. We are all connected to the energies that exist within and around us, to the natural flow. I have a point of knowledge and operation that is sometimes referred to as our conscious or intuition. These emotions originate from somewhere, which we refer to as spirituality.

> ### *Here's the Nugget*
>
> Teachers must be clear about their purpose; when they are, their passion flows and the learning space becomes a powerful environment for all.

Works Cited

Hammond, Z. (2014). *Culturally responsive teaching and the brain: Promoting authentic engagement and rigor among culturally and linguistically diverse students.* Corwin Press.

Muhammad, G. (2020). *Cultivating genius: An equity framework for culturally and historically responsive literacy.* Scholastic Teaching Resources.

Sullivan, Debra R. (2016). *Cultivating the Genius of Black Children: Strategies to Close the Achievement Gap in the Early Years.* Redleaf Press.

Sidorkin, Alexander M. (1999). *Beyond Discourse: Education, the Self, and Dialogue.* Albany: SUNY Press.

Ravitch, Diane. (2013). *Reign of Error: The Hoax of the Privatization Movement and the Danger to America's Public Schools.* New York: Knopf.

www.ingramcontent.com/pod-product-compliance
Lightning Source LLC
Chambersburg PA
CBHW050448010526
44118CB00013B/1739